WILL WE ALWAYS BE FRIENDS?

Copyright © 2024 by Elle Constantine

All rights reserved. No part of this book may be reproduced or used in any manner without written permission of the copyright owner except for the use of quotations in a book review.

First hardcover edition November 2024
Published by: BookBaby

Written by: Elle Constantine
Illustrated by: Lidia Rózio

ISBN: 979-8-35098-573-3

Ages 3-7

WILL WE ALWAYS BE FRIENDS?

Written by Elle Constantine

illustrated by Lidia Rózio

Once upon a time, in a cozy little village, there lived some friendly animals who became great friends.

They knew how important it was to say no drugs.
But it wasn't always this way. It took a smart cat named Leo to stand up and walk away from a friend who asked him to do drugs.

Not long ago, a sweet young cat named Leo lived in that village. Leo loved playing in the park and making new friends in his hometown.

One sunny afternoon, Leo ran into his friend Wally while playing in the park. They met at school and quickly became good friends.

But on this day, Wally was acting differently than usual. He talked about something strange and offered Leo some colorful pills that looked like candy.

He said it would make him feel great!

Leo said, "No, thank you. I don't want any," but Wally kept saying, "Come on, just try it once! It'll be fun!"

Leo got scared. He didn't want Wally not to like him. But, he remembered the stories his parents told him about the dangers of drugs and taking unknown things from not only strangers but even his friends.

They said it was dangerous because you never know what they are giving you or what it could be.

Leo knew he had to stop Wally from asking him to take something that could harm his body and mind.

This time, Leo said it even louder, capturing the attention of the other animals. "No, I do not want to try it. I don't want to do drugs".

Wally's smile turned into a frown,
and he slowly walked away.
Leo watched him as he left the park, knowing
he made the right decision not to do drugs.

When Leo got home, he told his parents what happened. They said, "True friends never ask each other to do things that could be harmful.
Saying no to drugs is important.
You did the right thing.
We are so proud of you."

From that day forward, Leo chose his friends carefully. He was sad he and Wally were no longer friends, but he knew having friends who did not do drugs was the right thing to do.

Leo and his friends went on to live their best lives. They went on lots of fun and healthy adventures together. They knew saying no to drugs would keep them safe, healthy, and free to explore the world around them.

And, just like Leo and his friends, you too will stand up and walk away from friends and others who want you to do drugs because you know they are bad for you. You will always say no to drugs!

Thank you for taking an active role in educating children about the dangers of drugs before the age of eight.
It is crucial for several reasons:

1. Brain Development: Early childhood is a key period for brain development. Understanding the impacts of drugs can help children make informed choices as their brains develop.

2. Prevention: Early education can instill a strong foundation against drug use, helping children recognize and resist peer pressure later on.

3. Critical Thinking: Teaching children about drugs encourages critical thinking skills and decision-making, enabling them to evaluate risks and consequences.

4. Informed Communication: Early discussions about drugs can create an open environment for communication, allowing children to feel comfortable discussing related topics with trusted adults.

5. Behavioral Influence: Early exposure to drug education can positively influence behaviors and attitudes towards substance use, leading to healthier choices in adolescence and adulthood.

By addressing these issues early, we can better equip children to navigate challenges related to substance use as they grow.